formatio

TRADITION. EXPERIENCE.
TRANSFORMATION.

Formatio books from InterVarsity Press follow the rich tradition of the church in the journey of spiritual formation. These books are not merely about being informed, but about being transformed by Christ and conformed to his image. Formatio stands in InterVarsity Press's evangelical publishing tradition by integrating God's Word with spiritual practice and by prompting readers to move from inward change to outward witness. InterVarsity Press uses the chambered nautilus for Formatio, a symbol of spiritual formation because of its continual spiral journey outward as it moves from its center. We believe that each of us is made with a deep desire to be in God's presence. Formatio books help us to fulfill our deepest desires and to become our true selves in light of God's grace.

 Spiritual Formation for Individuals and Groups

DISCOVERING SOUL CARE

MINDY CALIGUIRE

IVP Connect

An imprint of InterVarsity Press
Downers Grove, Illinois

InterVarsity Press
P.O. Box 1400, Downers Grove, IL 60515-1426
World Wide Web: www.ivpress.com
E-mail: email@ivpress.com

InterVarsity Press® is the book-publishing division of InterVarsity Christian Fellowship/USA®, a student movement active on campus at hundreds of universities, colleges and schools of nursing in the United States of America, and a member movement of the International Fellowship of Evangelical Students. For information about local and regional activities, write Public Relations Dept., InterVarsity Christian Fellowship/USA, 6400 Schroeder Rd., P.O. Box 7895, Madison, WI 53707-7895, or visit the IVCF website at <www.intervarsity.org>.

Design: Cindy Kiple
Images: chair: Ryan McVay/Getty Images
        chair icon: illustration by Kerri Liu

ISBN 978-0-8308-3509-6

Printed in the United States of America ∞

P   20   19   18   17   16   15   14   13   12   11   10   9   8   7
Y   23   22   21   20   19   18   17   16   15

CONTENTS

INTRODUCTION

Widely considered one of the most difficult marathons in the world, the Boston Marathon is for only the most elite runners. In fact, a qualifying time from another marathon is required even to enter the race. An infamous five-mile series of inclines toward the finish line starts at mile sixteen—right before runners hit "the wall." They call the last and longest of the hills "Heartbreak Hill."

In 1995, having just moved to Massachusetts with my husband to begin a new ministry, I had the opportunity to watch a portion of the Boston Marathon right around the corner from our apartment in Newton. We watched from the edge of Commonwealth Avenue, at about mile twenty—right at Heartbreak Hill—of the 26.2 mile race.

Jam-packed with onlookers, parties and bands, the crowds on the street had been waiting for hours in anticipation of the runners' arrival. But an expectant silence came over the crowd at the appearance of the helicopters overhead and media trucks heralding the arrival of the first competitors. The short-lived hush quickly shifted to wild cheering as the frontrunners appeared. These runners were practically sprinting, despite the distance already covered. They represented the top marathon runners in the world.

One of those frontrunners immediately caught my attention. The man was from Kenya, and he was part of the lead pack. But something was wrong—and soon, to our collective horror, we realized he was struggling to stay upright. The other runners swerved to avoid him; then the crowd on the side of the street parted. This pain-ridden athlete stumbled, then faltered over the curbside and collapsed on someone's front lawn.

Laying there on the grass, twitching violently, his eyes rolled back into their sockets, having lost control of his senses, I thought he was dying. We all watched in fear and silence as an emergency team located him, wrapped him in a foil survival blanket and whisked him away in an ambulance. Later we learned that he recovered and would be fine— but he was clearly not going to finish that race that day. He had lost the essential balance between an aggressive yet sustainable pace, and Heartbreak Hill had gotten the best of him.

As I watched that elite runner in April of 1995, I had no idea that I was headed for my own spiritual and emotional Heartbreak Hill. Like that marathoner, I too would push beyond my reserve and lose sustainability. And although I was a relatively accomplished ministry leader, I would also wind up twitching on the sidelines of my own life, desperate for someone to hand me a survival blanket and unsure whether I would ever compete again.

Thankfully I too have been restored to health and am able to run again. But I learned lessons from my collapse, lessons that fuel my desire to help people find a way of life, a way of *being,* that not only keeps them from falling out of the race but enables them to complete it.

Today I meet many people—often forerunners in their fields—who find themselves nearing exhaustion. They may not be on the sidelines or stumbling noticeably, but far too many are dangerously low on their reserves, running on fumes. Some are smack in the middle of their own spiritual Heartbreak Hill.

That may or may not be where you are today. If not, that's great! You may have noticed others on the sidelines and you don't want to end up there yourself, or maybe you can begin to feel the lactic acid building up in your soul. For you, this study can be "how *not* to head that way."

But if you identify with the fainting runner, then it is my prayer that the following pages—infused by God's Spirit—may serve as refreshing water for your thirsty soul. You have been running hard, and you've run a long way, but the end is nowhere in sight, and it may be uphill from here. Even so, there is hope for your soul!

Discovering Soul Care

Soul Care Resources is designed to be a simple, but not simplistic, guide to maintaining or recovering the life and health of your soul, that essential personhood created by God as *you*. To do that, we'll do assessments to discern the current health of your soul. We'll reflect on the reasons why your soul's health matters so much. Finally, we'll explore practical ways to restore life and vitality to your soul though authentic connection with God as Father, Son and Spirit—one step at a time.

This book is divided into four experiences—"Soul Health," "Soul Becoming," "Soul Care" and "Soul Decisions." Within each experience are four distinct parts that could be used as daily readings. Some parts are longer than others, so feel free to take more than a day to cover the material. Each part builds on the other, so you'll want to read one part at a time and reflect on the questions embedded in the text.

If daily readings aren't workable for you, just spending a day or two with each of the parts should allow you to comfortably complete one experience in a week, and the entire guide within about a month.

The fifth section of each part includes a discussion starter that you can use with a small group or friend if you wish.

Also available in the Soul Care Resources series is *Spiritual Friendship*. This guide will allow you to explore specific ways to care for your soul in companionship with others.

Are you ready to recover your reserves?

"Once we clearly acknowledge the soul,
we can learn to hear its cries."

DALLAS WILLARD, *RENOVATION OF THE HEART*

1 BEYOND SOUL NEGLECT

What has your soul been crying for lately? Do you know?

Some of us sense the soul's cries directly and immediately; most of us do not. And if those cries are at all painful, we are often tempted to avoid them entirely. Henri Nouwen observed, "There are two extremes to avoid: being completely absorbed in your pain and being distracted by so many things that you stay far from the wound you want to heal" (*The Inner Voice of Love*).

One factor that makes the voice of the soul so difficult to hear is that its cries come out sideways: through our emotions, our choices, our thoughts, our relationships and even our bodies. That's why we must learn to hear them. But we can learn!

One of the most helpful ways to become aware of these sideways symptoms is to ask ourselves: When my soul has been neglected, what tends to emerge? (Of course, we never *intend* to allow our soul's health to diminish—it's benign neglect!)

How do I think? Feel? Act? Relate? When my soul is healthy—aware of my connection with God in the moment and sure of his love for me—what flows out of me at those times? That is, what are the *symptoms* of soul health for me?

When I recently asked this question at a gathering, the two lists of symptoms were developed in a matter of minutes. It was easy to come up with the symptoms!

Often, symptoms of soul neglect include self-absorption, shame, apathy, toxic anger, physical fatigue, isolation, stronger temptation to sin, drivenness, feelings of desperation, panic, insecurity, callousness, a judgmental attitude, cynicism and lack of desire for God.

Some symptoms of soul health would be love, joy, compassion, giving and receiving grace, generosity of spirit, peace, ability to trust, discernment, humility, creativity, vision, balance and focus. Even our energy for work emerges naturally from the overflow of a deepening life with God.

We can spend a great deal of energy attempting to decrease the symptoms of soul neglect and attempting to increase the symptoms of soul health. But whenever we focus on the symptoms rather than the causes, the results are short-lived and perhaps even counterproductive. Why not focus on the source of the trauma, a neglected soul?

Now, when I talk about the soul, I am considering it in the context of our whole personhood. The soul is not to be separated from the body but is an integral part of who we are as people of both body and spirit. We tend to think of the soul only with reference to whether or not it is "saved" or "born again" or "heaven-bound." And while the eternal destiny of the soul is very important, something else is quite true about souls and vitally important in the here and now: Souls are living.

Like all living things, our souls can thrive or they can shrivel.

Our souls form the very foundation of who we are. In *Renovation of the Heart* Dallas Willard writes, "Fundamental aspects of life such as art, sleep, sex, ritual, family ('roots'), parenting, community, health, and meaningful work are all in fact soul functions, and they fail and fall apart to the degree that soul diminishes." Elsewhere he says, "When we speak of the human soul, then, we are speaking of the deepest level of life and power in the human being." No wonder God cares so much about the human soul!

Everything about our lives, about our personhood, is in some way a function of the soul. As Dallas Willard puts it (also in *Renovation of the Heart*), our soul is like the silent, invisible yet necessary Central Processing Unit (CPU) of our person. Our soul, and thus our soul's health, is the driving force behind everything that matters to us.

So what makes a soul healthy? Here's a clue: it's *not* related to our external circumstances.

Quite simply, *a soul is healthy to the extent that it maintains a strong connection and receptivity to God.* Under those conditions, the soul is most alive, most receptive to divine breathings, divine promptings and divine power in the face of joy or pain or opposition. Connection and receptivity—a rather simple spiritual concept, really.

Over the next days and weeks we will aim to uncover the truth about what's going on with our souls so that we can begin to experience God in new and restorative ways.

He refreshes my soul. (Psalm 23:3)

■ Return to the opening question and spend some time journaling your response. The answer to the question may not come quickly—or at all—but explore the thoughts and feelings it evokes. What has your soul been crying for lately?

2 ASSESSING SOUL HEALTH

What's the current state of your own soul? Using the list on page 14, and adding a few of your own, write down the symptoms of soul health and of soul neglect that you—or someone who knows you well—would say are true of you lately. You can use the chart on page 18. You'll most likely have a few of each, or maybe only one or the other. Whatever it is, be honest!

After you've completed the chart, take time to reflect on it. How do you *feel* about your assessment? As you look over these lists, take a moment to write down your response to your assessment. Do you resist it? Does it feel false? Hopeless? Desireable?

Living from a healthy soul does not mean you'll have an easy life where the bills are all paid, no one is sick and everything goes smoothly. Living from a healthy soul means you remain alive to God, alive to yourself and alive to others, smack in the middle of the ups and downs of life.

■ What circumstances in your life are most challenging right now?

My Symptoms of Soul Health

My Symptoms of Soul Neglect

■ What difference do you imagine a deeper sense of connection with God would bring to these circumstances, even if nothing else changed? Try to be as specific as you can.

Before moving on, take a moment to talk to God about these specific circumstances and your desire to remain connected to his truth, goodness, compassion, power or whatever else comes to mind.

■ What do you most need to receive from God right now? Go ahead and ask for what you most want, whether it's a sense of joy, or a nap, or forgiveness, or encouragement, or clarity on a decision, or more peace, or restoration of a "first love."

Read Psalm 145:16-19 below.

> *You open your hand*
> *and satisfy the desires of every living thing.*
>
> *The LORD is righteous in all his ways*
> *and faithful in all he does.*
>
> *The LORD is near to all who call on him,*
> *to all who call on him in truth.*
>
> *He fulfills the desires of those who fear him;*
> *he hears their cry and saves them.*

■ How do you find yourself responding to God in this psalm?

Let these times of reflection be a place in which you call on him in truth.

So what's actually going on when a soul becomes healthy? Let's take a look inside the process of spiritual transformation.

Souls constantly change in shape and form. Every person you've ever laid eyes on has a body— and also a soul. But not all souls are the same, nor are they at the same stage of being formed. Dallas Willard writes in *Renovation of the Heart,* "Terrorists as well as saints have had a spiritual formation." Spiritual formation, at its core then, is not some class we sign up for or an activity we *do* but a basic fact of human existence—our souls are always being formed.

When we enter into a right relationship with God our souls are forever changed. Many of us can consciously mark a turning point, or series of points, when we actively accepted God's grace and his forgiveness. We connected in a real relationship with God at some irreplaceable "point A." A new birth to authentic spiritual life began then for us. But just as in physical life, new birth begins life. It doesn't complete it. The soul isn't done yet.

In Galatians 4:19, the apostle Paul writes a letter to a community of Christians, challenging them to seek more accurate thinking and a more intentional life by grace—but not by rule keeping and religiosity. Tenderly referring to his recipients as "dear children," Paul expresses his own ardent concern that they prioritize their spiritual development by describing his deep desire for them to be formed in Christ as being like "the pains of childbirth."

As a spiritual mentor, Paul knew the process of transformation and wanted the Galatians to understand it as well. Christ would be formed in them. The aim wasn't just to get what they needed *from* God but to become something *for* God. Likewise, you weren't meant to stay the person you are right now; you were meant for something more. You have room to grow—and that's a good thing. You were made to be something more. It's worth being, and becoming, that person.

■ From what you understand, what kind of character qualities did Christ demonstrate when he was on Earth?

■ What would it mean for those qualities to be "formed" in someone?

■ Do you see this kind of growth as very important in your life? Why or why not?

Ultimately the clearest way to express what God's character is like is in just one word: *love*. Though too few of us set New Year's resolutions to become more loving, that goal really does create the best way of being. The "us" five years from now should be a more loving us.

Of course, the contemporary word *love* gets overused and misses the point. The kind of God-formed love is not a weak, spineless love, easily swayed to lose its identity and unable to say "no" to anything or anyone. Instead, those who develop this kind of love become purpose-filled and spiritually powerful people who shake the earth and instill in the hearts of others a sense of their own value.

The outcome of our "spiritual formation" isn't about becoming unworldly, mystical or monkish. It's not about attending church meetings. Instead, it's to become more Christlike. It's to become someone who people would describe in ways such as "I always feel loved when I'm around them" or "I never doubt they love me."

When we have entered into a relationship with God, we change from the *inside out*. The Holy Spirit works constantly to encourage, to challenge, to heal, to restore, to convict and to guide us toward being fully formed. When the life of God gets in our souls, the Spirit of God takes on the function of transforming agent inside us. Although we can't fully know or understand how this works, or when this is happening, we do know this: "Being confident of this, that he who began a good work in you will carry it on to completion" (Philippians 1:6).

Notice a key word in Philippians 1:6: *confident*. The God of the universe makes a unilateral, unconditional, no-holds-barred commitment to your spiritual growth. He promises he will continue his work in you—and so strong is his promise that he urges you, through Paul's words, to be confident of this, to rest securely in that certainty!

God does not say that if you just "straighten up and fly right" he'll help you. Nor does he say that "once you get your whole act together" he'll do his part. No! He *will* complete his work. You need not be the star performer or the superspiritual to get God to contribute. His power generously flows toward screwups, spiritual beginners *and* spiritual giants.

■ As you think of your present relationship with God, what words would you use to describe your level of confidence that God is at work in you right now? (For example: sort of; not sure; great concept but never experienced it, and so on. Be careful not to describe merely what you should feel based on what you know, but what you actually feel based on your relationship.)

■ Have you recently sensed God's activity in your life? If so, how? If not, why might that be?

One final thought about the process of transformation: As powerful and good as God is, nothing will happen unless you also take an active role in the process of transformation. Just a few short paragraphs beyond the promise of God's work in our lives, we read this: "work out your salvation with fear and trembling" (Philippians 2:12).

What does "work out" mean if not "Don't just sit there, do something"? For one, these words make clear that we work *out* our salvation; we need not work *for* our salvation. The issue of our eternal relationship with God has been settled by Jesus' death on the cross and his resurrection. It's not about earning God's love and forgiveness. In relationship with Jesus, we've got that. But once that seed of grace has been planted deep within our souls, there is effort we expend to work it out—to press it through.

While God doesn't hack off all of our rough edges right away, we can be confident—absolutely sure—that God *is* at work in us. For the rest of our lives, we are responsible for allowing God's grace to be infused in our souls and letting him spread it through to every dimension of life.

■ Imagine on paper: What would a more loving "you" be like? Be specific.

■ Restate here your understanding of God's part in forming and transforming your inner person:

The effort we expend toward the goal of Christ being formed in us is essential. But what exactly is the work that we do? And how might we do it in our busy, ordinary or what often feels like unspiritual, everyday lives?

Though God is always at work (even at this very moment, while you read!), what fluctuates is our openness and receptivity. All God's goodness, power, wisdom and love await and remain as nothing but potential until the human soul "cracks" and allows the transformation to occur. While we may be in relationship with God, we can unconsciously remain closed to this transformational work in our lives. Just look around—or look inside.

Consider why you are reading this book. The fact that you chose to engage in this study most likely means you really do want to experience all the love and transformation God has for you. You may realize you're not "done just yet," and you would like to craft a way of life that opens you up to more genuine spiritual living. Perhaps you would like to carve out time, space and even energy from your days in order to cultivate openness and receptivity to God's activity in you and all around you. Your intentions are probably good. So what's next?

For most of us, our experience of "churchgoing" or "religion" may have meant getting more knowledge about God. As important as that is, the next vital shift for most of us is moving from seeking to know more *about* God to becoming fully available and present *with* God. That's no small shift—especially if we've been doing things the other way for most of our lives.

Moving from knowing a lot about God to really knowing God is foundational to our spiritual formation. It's one thing to know a whole lot about our spouses, our children or our friends. It's something quite different to know *them*. To really know someone requires willingness to go way beyond the gathering of data points and facts (though these are important as well). But the deeper knowing is connecting being to being. It's developing rapport, growing in respect or familiarity, and it requires time, attention and willingness to listen, not just speak. Life-giving relationships hinge more on knowing than knowing about.

How much more this is true in our relationships with God. The seventeenth-century French monk known to us as Brother Lawrence still speaks to us in his little book called *The Practice of the Presence of God*. The main message of this classic is that at any moment and in any circumstance, the soul that seeks God may find him. It is possible to practice the presence of God. Lawrence, through his simple activities, revealed it was possible to see God's hand in every facet of his life. He wrote, "The time of business does not with me differ from the time of prayer, and in the noise and clatter of my kitchen . . . I possess God in as great tranquility as if I were upon my knees at the blessed sacrament."

Just like Brother Lawrence, the way we become present and open with God in everyday life is through what are traditionally referred to as spiritual practices. Spiritual practices are things we *do*—with great levels of intentionality—to pay attention to and be receptive to the ongoing work of God in our lives. They are practices aimed at nurturing a relationship with God at all times. This is *our* part in the "working out of our salvation."

Spiritual practices come in all sizes and shapes and are as unique and individual as the persons seeking a deeper connection with God. What makes something effective as a practice is its ability to open the soul authentically to God—to help break down or crack through our defenses.

Three expressions of spiritual practices are important:

(1) PUBLIC EXPRESSIONS. These are times of prayer, worship or teaching with a large group of people (anywhere from dozens to even thousands of people) where we experience something of God that forever transforms who we are as people.

■ Many people can think of times when they experienced God powerfully and transformationally in that kind of setting—how about you? Jot down a few words that describe a time when you sensed God moving in your soul during a large group experience of some kind.

(2) PERSON-TO-PERSON EXPRESSIONS. There are times when our soul "cracks" and we allow God to do a new thing because of our interactions with others—whether in a formal small group or simply in our relationships. In those times, God chooses to reveal something new, to heal a past wound, to spark a new vision through the eyes, ears, voice

or hands of another person. And so we arrange our lives accordingly—we develop those relationships not only for the fun and joys of companionship but also because we expect to hear something of God in our friends that we would not experience otherwise.

■ If you have experienced this kind of relationship, jot down the names of a few people through whom God has worked powerfully in your life.

(3) PRIVATE EXPRESSIONS. There are also ways that God interacts with his people very personally and individually. These kinds of spiritual practices are just between you and God, and the solitary nature is part of the power of the practice. Examples could be times of a prayerful walk in nature, simplicity, journaling, silence, praying or reading Scripture.

■ What practices have you pursued on your own?

■ Which practices seem to fuel your soul most deeply or directly?

Whatever form they take, *spiritual practices can bring you to a place of openness with God*. They are the intentionality and effort involved in "working out our salvation." That's how you care for your soul. It's that simple and it's that hard. And whose job is it? Many people feel overwhelmed by their circumstances, unable to care for their souls because of others' demands, the pressing needs of the day or the limits of time. Some even look to others, thinking someone else should care for their souls.

However, you will need to take responsibility for your own soul care. The care of your soul is not your spouse's job, your employer's job, your children's job or even, in the end, your church's job. It's great if those external forces are cooperative. But only you can choose openness.

For example when we attend church, it's not really about whether we like the worship style or music or whether the preaching is relevant. When we show up with open souls, God will meet us. Sometimes we may feel empty, restless or uninterested. Still, we can ask, "What is God saying to me?" And then we choose how we respond.

These are questions for the soul.

And the choice is yours.

■ Take a few minutes to reflect on a recent time you opened your soul to God. Where were you and what were you doing?

■ What observations can you make about why you were open at that time?

5 GROUP DISCUSSION

Summary

Our souls are living, and like any other living things they require nourishment in order to thrive. Without nourishment, the symptoms of soul neglect will be expressed. What brings life to the soul, though, is open and authentic connection with God. When that connection is as it should be, the soul naturally expresses the life of God within it and is thus open to the transformational work of God in the deepest parts. God is always active in the process of lovingly shaping our inner person to be more like Christ, ultimately marked by love. And yet we too play a role in that transformation process. Our part is to learn ways of bringing the soul to a place of openness with God—often referred to as "spiritual practices." Whether in the context of large group settings, interpersonal settings or even alone by ourselves, the effort and intentionality of opening our souls to God is the essential part we play in order for God's life to have full expression in and through ours. Those spiritual practices, whatever form they take, represent ways we can care for our souls and thus experience the kind of life God has made available to all of his people. But the choice is ours. Will we arrange our lives to experience it or not? Our soul's symptoms invariably reveal our choice.

Discussion Basics

This discussion guide works best in a context of openness and vulnerability among friends (new or old!). As such, a few ground rules are in order.[1]

First, please feel no pressure to answer any of these questions. We'd encourage you to be vulnerable, but if at any time for any reason you don't feel comfortable, it's OK to take a pass.

Second, please give one another the gift of listening, not advice. This is not the time to tell about when that same thing happened to you or about the Scripture verse that "solves" that problem. Ask a follow-up question perhaps, or simply remain quiet. But refrain from interjecting your own advice.

Third, no faking. There is no need to be anything other than who you are. If what's really true feels too uncomfortable to talk about, just take a pass. Trust in the process of authentic, vulnerable communication with God and others.

And last, ruthlessly protect and honor one another's confidentiality. When a friend shares an intimate struggle or concern, it represents a gift of their trust in us. We can even thank them! But it was given to us, not to everyone we know, so we guard our words accordingly.

Opening

If you don't know each other already, take plenty of time to share names and some basic get-to-know-you information like where you live, what kind of work you do, what your family is like, and maybe something silly like your favorite childhood cartoon or book. Then proceed to the question below.

What brought you to want to do this study at this time in your life?

---

[1]Adapted from *An Ordinary Day with Jesus* by John Ortberg and Ruth Haley Barton.

Discussion

1. What, if anything, did you sense God stirring in you through this first experience?

2. Go back over your written responses to parts one through four. What one or two ideas stand out as something you'd like to bring to the group? Why did they stand out to you?

3. Return to the "Soul Health Assessment" in part two. Share with the group some of the current symptoms of soul health or neglect that you've been experiencing. How did you feel about that assessment when you first did it? How do you feel about it now?

4. How do you respond to the idea that cultivating your soul's health is your own responsibility?

5. Read Philippians 1:6. Describe a time when you felt quite sure or confident of God's transformational activity in your life. When was a time you wished you had sensed it more directly?

6. Talk about one thing that you anticipate might be a challenge for you personally in the coming days or weeks. What might a more "loving" you in that situation or relationship look like?

Prayer

If you feel comfortable, close by praying for one another.

> *I keep asking that the God of our Lord Jesus Christ, the glorious Father, may give you the Spirit of wisdom and revelation, so that you may know him better. I pray that the eyes of your heart may be enlightened in order that you may know the hope to which he has called you, the riches of his glorious inheritance in his people, and his incomparably great power for us who believe. (Ephesians 1:17-19)*

■ Before the next gathering, complete "Experience Two: Soul Becoming." You might want to exchange basic contact information such as telephone numbers and email addresses.

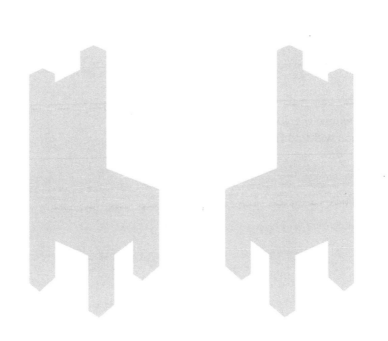

"Ask where the good way is, and walk in it,
and you will find rest for your souls."

JEREMIAH 6:16

EXPERIENCE TWO / *Soul Becoming*

1 NAVIGATING THE GAP

In the western world we are immersed in a culture that is obsessed with the idea that we can become something better than we are. Transformation is a billion-dollar industry. We hire executive coaches, management consultants, personal trainers, therapists, cosmetic surgeons and even supernannies to make our organizations or ourselves better, to transform us. We purchase Pilates tapes, organic food, multivitamins, age-defying creams, special diets and at-home gym equipment. Self-help books make bestseller lists, and celebrities of their authors. The newest top-rated television shows no longer reveal lifestyles of the rich and famous, but instead the lives of ordinary people who get to transform their homes, their looks, their children or their marriages—with a little help of course!

■ What's the most ridiculous product or service claim promising the buyer transformation of some sort that you've heard?

One thing's for sure: we long for improvement. We long to shed the emptiness, the ugliness and the ordinariness of our lives for beauty, fulfillment and meaning. We want to grow, to become, to fulfill our potential, to be free from whatever holds us back—even if what's holding us back is *us*. But how do you get free from yourself in order for your self to be free?

Jesus Christ offers a way through the conundrum. Die to yourself, and you'll fully live. The old can be made new; you can become a "new creation." This is good news! We are not forever doomed by our bad choices, our foolish mistakes, our deepest regrets.

But this "new creation" business has both a *now* and a *not yet* dimension to it. *Now* we have been brought into full relationship with God. Immediate. But the *not yet* part describes the person we will become as we mature and grow, as we are transformed.

I often think that when I raise the possibility of authentic, real change that I'm stepping on a potential hornet's nest of pain for most people. The reality is, many of us long ago gave up hope that we could actually become someone new. The invitation to hope again reawakens the reality of that pain, of that awareness of all that is not as it should be or could be. We are *not* what we could be, and it hurts.

My church describes the "destination" for spiritual growth as becoming a "fully devoted follower." I absolutely love the intensity of that phrase and its deep roots in church history and doctrine. But I also struggled with the idea. As I understood it, the term urged me to set my target on the "me" that was perfectly like Jesus. But if that is my goal, then no matter how much transformation I experience during my lifetime, I will never be that picture of perfection. I will always fail.

What a heavy burden for well-meaning Christ-followers to bear, never being "good enough."

We may come into a relationship with God in part through the joy and freedom of finally being accepted and loved unconditionally—finally being *good enough* on the basis of Jesus' love and sacrifice. But as good as that is, it doesn't take long for that perspective to revert. Once again we find ourselves under impossibly heavy burdens that Jesus never meant for us to bear. He said he came that we might have life, not that we'd be perfect.

Then one day, a friend helped me understand that full devotion is a matter of the heart, not a matter of moral or spiritual achievement. "The heart is what has the capacity to be devoted, Mindy," she said. "In fact, someone could be fully devoted on the day they became a Christian!" I remember thinking, *That's not widely known! How can that be true?*

When full devotion describes a quality of heart, it can be true at any stage of our spiritual development. It allows both for someone fresh in the faith and calls seasoned Christ-followers toward a lifetime of ongoing growth and transformation. *Full devotion is a state of our hearts when our understanding of truth is equal to our level of surrender.* When that equilibrium is reached, those incremental, irrevocable transactions take place, by God's hand, to transform the human soul. Authentic transformation happens, and human souls actually bear a greater and greater resemblance to God.

This part of our Soul Care guide addresses the very real possibility of transformation and how a person who pursues full devotion can actually experience it.

■ Why do you think the hope that we can become something more exists at all? Why is it such a powerful and universal desire?

■ How do you feel about working with this topic over the next few days?

What's the widest gap you've ever stood by? The Grand Canyon? A stone quarry? A coastline? Each of us experiences a gap between who we are and who we hope to be one day, and each of us responds to that gap differently.

For example, I am often painfully aware that I am not the kind of mother I would like to be. I am not as patient with my children's imperfections as I should be. I am not as aware of or concerned about their needs as I could be, nor am I selfless in serving them.

When I look at my work life, I find that I am never as organized as I could be. I don't follow up and complete projects with as much determination as I wish I would. I even find myself making the same mistakes in judgment again and again.

Some of these areas of weakness, such as lack of organizational skills, represent nothing more or less than my personality—the particular way in which I have been made by God. But others are more directly related to the quality of my character.

I have a good sense of what my life on "this side" of my gap looks like. It doesn't take me long to put together a list that identifies all the ways I'm not measuring up. I also have a sense of what my life on the other side of the gap—the perfect version, or at least one that's a whole lot better—would look like. How about you?

Think for a moment about this gap as it exists in your own life. Jot down some responses to the following questions:

■ List a few facets of your life in which the gap is most pronounced. Consider finances, physical fitness, relationships, career and so on. Write a bit about your highest hopes for those areas.

■ How do you tend to respond to that gap when you think about it? (Do you ignore it? get angry? feel frustrated? hopeless? guilty? shameful? blame it on someone else?)

Initially, in the freshness and naiveté of a new relationship with God, we might simply start doing what we've done in other areas of our lives before—get a clear picture of the destination, and map out the path to achievement. I know I did! During my sophomore year at Cornell, over Christmas break I learned that God desired for his children to exhibit nine hallmark qualities of his Spirit—the fruit of the Spirit—listed in Galatians 5:22.

That next semester, back at school, I charted out my development plan accordingly. January would be about love, February would be about peace, March would cover joy, and by April I'd be ready for patience! Month by month, I'd "tackle" each of these fruits just like I approached my calculus curriculum.

Needless to say, by April's end it was clear I had missed something. There simply was no discernable progress, and in fact it appeared I was worse off for my "efforts" because I was more aware than before just how wide the gap actually was.

When we face this gap between who we are and who we might become, when we realize we cannot cross it in our own power, we are tempted to move in one of two directions: hypocrisy or despair. Many take the path of hypocrisy—of pretending. On this path we create an illusion of transformation by rigid behavior management and rule keeping. We "bump" up into our heads and conduct our relationship with God and others from that place, where what we know suffices and makes up for the lack of who we have (or have not) become.

The other alternative is perhaps a tad more authentic, but not much more appealing. We move in despair and hopelessness that we will ever change and begin to hate our selves deeply.

There are several reasons why these gaps remain in our lives. For example, Scripture (and common sense) tells us the gap could be a result of our own foolish choices—bad decisions that have landed us in adverse circumstances. For some people, the gap exists in part because their standards for themselves are too high—impossible demands. These people might be overachieving perfectionists and only see the places where they fall short of perfection. Others have an incorrect vision of the person they're supposed to become in the first place, so their gap-management is complicated by the fact that they're actually working against the way God intended for them to be.

■ Can you identify with any of these reasons for the gap in your own life? Which ones, and why?

While each of these reasons for the gap are valid and could be at work in your life, there is one other important reason to consider: God's protection and love. Have you ever thought of that before? God certainly has the power to instantly, dramatically transform us, but typically he doesn't. The pattern we most often observe in Scripture involves a process—a joint, lifelong venture between us and him, which can only happen when we allow God space to walk alongside us.

The book of Exodus records a curious story that depicts this pattern of God's working with people in process. In this passage, the people of God stand on a very significant threshold in their development as a nation: they are about to enter the Promised Land! And just like the promise given to us in Philippians 1:6, God clearly communicates his commitment to use all the power necessary to bring the Israelites into their future destiny.

Read Exodus 23:20, 27-28, below, and as you read, give a little "woo-hoo!" every time you hear God promise to act on his people's behalf.

See, I am sending an angel ahead of you to guard you along the way and to bring you to the place I have prepared. . . .

I will send my terror ahead of you and throw into confusion every nation you encounter. I will make all your enemies turn their backs and run. I will send the hornet ahead of you to drive the Hivites, Canaanites and Hittites out of your way.

Can't you just hear the people thinking or saying *"Woo-hoo!"* every time they hear how God will make the victory sure? But the next two verses must have thrown a bit of a wet blanket on the whole affair.

What does God say next? Listen closely; this gives us a picture of God's heart toward the process of human transformation.

But I will not drive them out in a single year, because the land would become desolate and the wild animals too numerous for you. Little by little I will drive them out before you, until you have increased enough to take possession of the land. (Exodus 23:29-30)

■ Look back to these verses—what reasons does God give for the "process approach" to fulfilling the Israelites' destiny?

In this new land, the Israelites would encounter enemies they couldn't even dream of, and they would be at great risk. How would God prepare them to fulfill their destiny? One day at a time. One new baby at a time. One healthy marriage at a time. One functioning farm at a time. One flock of sheep at a time. One small victory at a time. Until they have increased enough to take possession. *Process.*

The ultimate outcome sounds lovely, but can you imagine what that felt like in the interim? Might they have felt like they were failing? Might they have felt like they were incompetent? Might they even have felt hopeless, like they would never experience what God had for them? But had God stopped working? Was he abandoning them midway through? No.

How does this relate to us today? When we look at transformation, we're faced with the gap. We're faced with where we are now and what our destiny, our future or personal "Promised Land" will be.

The fact of the gap in your life is not a crisis. Far from failure on your part, the gap may merely be the protection of a loving God who never loses sight of who he has uniquely designed you to both be and become. He's more concerned that it come to pass, in fact, than you are.

What can become a crisis is how you respond to that gap.

Maybe there's a way to look beyond the gap and see something else. We'll explore that possibility in part three.

3 SEEING THE PATH OF TRUTH AND SURRENDER

What if we set our sights on something besides the other side of the gap—on something other than the impossible goal of perfection?

A clue for us lies in our new picture of a fully devoted heart—a heart whose understanding of truth correlates to its level of surrender.

When someone begins a relationship with God, they experience this equilibrium of full devotion. They came to understand some truths about God, about themselves and about the invitation of forgiveness being offered. And whether the process of accepting that invitation happened in an instant or during a lengthy season, eventually their level of surrender came in line with their understanding of those truths. They were fully devoted; their heart was as devoted as it knew to be.

But from that day forward, for the rest of our lives, there is an ongoing growth process during which we become aware of new truths— truths about God, truths about ourselves or truths about the world around us. And there will be an ongoing wrestling between our will and these new truths as we surrender. And when we do surrender in light of whatever particular area of truth, our hearts are once again fully devoted and we have become something new. We surrender and change gradually, perhaps, but we are nonetheless new.

What would some real-life examples of this be? Here are a few:

God is concerned for the poor. When we grasp this truth, if we are fully devoted, our lives will eventually surrender to that truth. Our time, checkbooks and activities will actually reflect the same concern God has. Our understanding of truth and our level of surrender will be in line with one another.

God cares about the way we handle finances. What does God say about money? Do we know? And once we do, do we "surrender" to it? Do we start living that way? This is typically a process of learning about what God has to say about earning, about spending, about saving, about giving, about the place money has in our lives. What does surrendering over time to those truths look like? Whatever it may look like, it paints the picture of a fully devoted heart when the truth gets pressed into how we live.

We are to forgive as we have been forgiven. When we grasp this truth, if we are pursuing full devotion, we will be exploring past wounds and doing the hard work of forgiveness as God enables. The imperative to forgive is seen throughout Scripture and is highlighted in Jesus' instructions to us on prayer (Matthew 6:9-13). But knowing how and even why to forgive is not the same as actually forgiving an offender. Being fully devoted means that we press this truth into how we live. Again, our level of understanding will be commensurate with our level of surrender.

Some truths are especially tricky to surrender to. One truth many of Jesus' people carry around in their heads and believe fervently is this:

We are fully loved, fully known and fully accepted by the God of the universe. What would life be like if we surrendered to this truth, allowing it to become more than head knowledge? if we lived in such a way that this truth influenced, as it necessarily would, every area of our lives? How would that play out in our relationships? who we are at work? the way we treat our bodies?

When you pursue having your heart be fully devoted to God, you will wrestle with God's heart about everything that matters to him, including you. He's fighting for your heart!

The list of qualities I've just taken you through is not designed to be an outline of next steps for you to follow in your particular spiritual journey. Instead my hope is that the examples I've given will help you to discover the big picture of how truth and surrender can line up in your life. When they do, the heart is devoted—as devoted as it knows to be. When they don't, it's not.

Of course, grasping these truths on a soul-level is not an easy process. It's not as simple as just reading a book or two and suddenly moving to the next level of "fully-devotedness." Grasping these truths takes a willingness to do the hard work of really considering Christ's claims and his call on our lives, and then fully surrendering to that truth and his will. So let's stop and reflect a bit on your journey with God up to this point.

■ Can you think of some examples of truths you've learned about God? Write one or two of them down.

■ What truths about yourself have you become aware of in the past? They could include truths about an attitude you've been carrying, or truths about your gifts and talents, or truths about your past that you need to "own."

■ What did it look like to surrender to these truths?

■ How did you come to the point of being willing to surrender?

As you can see, there are innumerable truths that God might impress on our hearts at any given time. Each of us has a different history, different character flaws, different talents and gifts to develop, and a different calling or destiny. Therefore, no one can establish a formula that says, "God always works on our compassion first, then our forgiveness, then our finances and then our sense of being loved." But we all face precisely the same challenges when it comes to truth and surrender: Am I open to new truths about God? about myself? about the world around me? Am I cultivating the kind of heart that is increasingly *willing* to surrender?

When we identify a new area of growth—a growth edge—we are wise to divert energy there rather than try to forge a different path based upon an artificial "growth map" that we or anyone else might impose on our spiritual journey. If we respond to God as he makes us aware of these areas for growth, we will become exactly who he has in mind for this season—and then the next, and then the next.

I find this understanding of a fully devoted heart gives us something both to reach for and something to rest in.

- The *reach* is in the pursuit and openness to truth and the work of surrender. We are active in the process, reaching for what is next in the journey.

• It also gives us something to finally *rest* in. We can rest our heads on the pillow at night and lovingly whisper, "God, you have my heart. I'm as surrendered as I know to be. There may be a new area for us to work on when I wake up tomorrow, but you have my heart." Truth and surrender are in concert with one another.

Sure, there will be numerous areas of our lives that will remain imperfect, but God is not asking us to work on all of those at once. When he does ask us to work on them, we hope and trust that we will. But for now, there is no condemnation, no fear of failure, no hesitation in taking the rest of the journey as it comes. There is full devotion, and at the same time, there is rest.

So how do we identify a growth edge? I'm guessing that as you've been reading this a few areas have been coming to mind—not necessarily because you're aware of how imperfect you are in those areas but because you sensed God nudging you about something recently. God's nudge may have come through a particular song, a passage of Scripture that has kept coming to mind, a topic that keeps coming up, a nagging feeling of anxiety or a struggle that keeps recurring.

■ What do you think your growth edge is?

■ What is a current area of truth that you're becoming aware of?

■ How have you become aware of that truth?

■ What would surrendering to that truth look like right now?

Full devotion is that state of your heart where your understanding of truth is equal to your level of surrender. This is a lifelong target, a dynamic target. It's always moving; we're always responding. That's relationship.

Spiritual growth and intimacy with God do not come from a self-directed spiritual improvement plan based on an objective analysis of the goal of perfection and our current position in relation to that goal. The gap cannot be traversed. In some ways, for our own protection, we may not be ready to cross that bridge completely. Instead, spiritual growth and intimacy with God are cultivated by attending to what's current between us and God. Full devotion occurs when we pursue new truths about God, ourselves and life, and when we remain open to surrender in those areas.

5 GROUP DISCUSSION

Summary

It seems nearly everyone in our world is eager to experience transformation. Most of us can imagine the kind of person we wish we were—the kind of improvements we'd like to experience in our families, careers, appearance, and even personality or character. And in the Christian life, the hope for actual transformation, at the very core of who we are, is real! God has promised, and is already at work to accomplish, just such a transformation within us. But what path should we take as we attempt to traverse the impossible gap between who we are right now and the person we are becoming? Rather than the path of self-improvement, even spiritual self-improvement, the path of full devotion is a steady and reliable one. A fully devoted heart is open to truth and is surrendered. A fully devoted heart can recognize the current activity of God and respond. Rather than a lifetime of never being "good enough," a life of full devotion urges us to pay attention to what's current and focus our energies there. We can safely trust that God will lead the process of transformation in our lives at the pace and in the sequence that best serves his purposes for our overall development.

Opening

How have you been doing since we last gathered as a group? Have you felt closer to or more distant from God lately? Why?

Discussion

1. What, if anything, did you sense God stirring in you through this second experience?

2. Go back over your written responses to parts one through four. What one or two ideas stand out as something you'd like to bring to the group? Why did they stand out to you?

3. Return to part two, "Seeing the Gap." Talk about your responses to the questions in this section.

4. You may find that passage of Scripture can represent "the gap" for you. For some people, it may be the Beatitudes in Matthew 5, or for others the fruit of the Spirit in Galatians 5. For others it might be 1 Corinthians 13. Share it with the group if you feel comfortable. *Why* do you think you are especially challenged by that passage?

5. What happens in a person or in a community when truth and sur-render are out of balance? For example, when someone possesses great quantities of "truth" but is unwilling to surrender? What if there was a strong sense of surrender without truth?

6. How does the concept of a growth edge fit with your understanding and experience of life with God?

Prayer

If you feel comfortable, close by praying for one another.

Before the next gathering, complete "Experience Three: Soul Care."

"I have calmed myself
    and quieted my ambitions;
    I am like a weaned child with its mother;
    like a weaned child I am content."

PSALM 131:2

EXPERIENCE THREE / *Soul Care*

1 THE TWO CHAIRS

Transformation can be a long, slow process. But, make no mistake, when God moves in a human soul, it changes. A transaction of sorts is underway. Just as transactions in your bank account fundamentally change the nature of what's there, spiritual transactions have that same quality. They may be difficult to discern, but they are real.

Just as transactions in your bank account fundamentally change the nature of what's there, spiritual transactions have that same quality. They may be difficult to discern, but they are real.

When transactions take place in the business world, there are generally two or more parties who "come to the table." Picture yourself sitting at a table with God. What's on the table here is your soul's transformation. For health to be restored and for transformation to occur, both you and God will need to bring something to the table. What unique qualities will God contribute to what the team (you and him) needs to accomplish? The list is quite extensive, of course:

• power to change a human soul

• complete understanding of why things are the way they are

- compassion to look on the truth of who we are with eyes of love
- vision for us and the purpose for which he's made us
- wisdom to see the past, the now, the future, as well as the path between here and there
- forgiveness for our sin
- delight in us and in our process

God is not some stern ruler who's impatiently waiting for us to "get it right." Instead, God is the loving, powerful lover of our souls who sits in that chair at all times, in all circumstances, offering what he and only he can bring to the table of transformation. And he brings quite a bit.

■ When you think of the idea of what God "brings to the table" in your soul's restoration, what is most appealing to you right now?

■ In what ways has he already brought those things into your life?

■ What is it that you feel you still need?

Now how about us? What do we bring? Not much by comparison, for sure. But bring it we must, or the deal won't go through. Several words could describe it, but a good one would be this: *openness*. We bring openness, a willingness to let God do what only he can do in our heart. Other ways to say it would be that we bring humility, yieldedness or brokenness. But the main idea is we basically bring ourselves, and we bring ourselves open. This is critical. God is a respecter of persons; he will not barge through the boundaries of our interior world uninvited. Just as he refrains from forcing anyone into relationship with him in the first place, God will not force you to receive his love and nurture and presence.

If the transformation that your soul so desperately needs and that God is so eager to provide is going to happen, you have to actually sit down in that chair at the table. Then you'll need to stop squirming and get quiet in that chair—and lean in to hear the One sitting across from you.

Seems pretty small, doesn't it? Amazingly though, sitting down in your chair can be very difficult to do. Rather than actually sitting down to be with God, many people spend far too much time in the general vicinity where God is but refuse to sit down, preferring instead to incessantly run tiresome laps around the room, bustling about with all kinds of "virtuous" activities, slapping the Almighty a high-five every once in a while as they pass by.

No question, we're made to run—we're made to exert and accomplish and contribute and work and serve and lead. But we're also made to connect, to receive, to be transformed, to be loved. And as God has designed the spiritual life, we're designed to do all that accomplishing out of the overflow of the connecting, not the reverse.

■ What will it take for you to actually stop running and just sit down and listen? (For example, how might you need to adjust your schedule?)

■ What will it take for you to get quiet?

How do you respond to the idea of spending time with God? Is this an appealing idea? Or does it sound boring? Does it feel like being sent to the principal's office? Or does it sound like spending time at a coffee shop with a friend?

When God sits in the opposite chair waiting to meet with us, who is it that awaits? It helps to anchor our understanding of "what God brings" in Scripture. In order to do this, look up the verses listed on the next page to help focus on that picture more clearly.

■ In the space provided in the chart on the next page, answer the question "In general, what does God bring?" Then note the specific word or phrase in each passage that you most desire today.

Text	What Does God Bring?	What Do I Desire?
Exodus 15:26		
Psalm 103		
Matthew 11:29		
1 John 4:7, 16		
1 Corinthians 13		

After you have completed the chart, read through 1 Corinthians 13 again, knowing that this is how God, who is perfect love, loves you.

Some of us are unaware that God implicitly invites us to sit down in that chair, so we never actually do. The business of life keeps us running, but in truth we were unaware that Jesus might just want to be with us. Others of us know we "should" spend time with God, but it can feel forced and contrived. Our time with God can become less about the relationship and a loving work of transformation than it is about how hard we might study or how long we might pray. More achievement.

Unfortunately, sometimes even in the midst of our otherwise spiritual activities, we can still be running laps around the room rather than internally sitting quietly to receive from God. Perhaps we don't want to give up control and actually sit down, or maybe we are afraid of what will come up for us internally if we were to get truly quiet. Sometimes we're sitting down and quiet, but our arms are folded and we're turned away from God. We don't really want to hear or receive what God has to say.

Make no mistake—even under those circumstances this God of ours loves us. But he doesn't only love us as we are; he loves us with intention and desire for our freedom, for the good purposes for which he designed us to be fulfilled.

■ If you could imagine yourself in God's place—in his chair—what do you think he'd want to say to you right now?

One of the most tragic verses comes to us from God by the hand of his prophet Isaiah. In Isaiah 30:15 we are told:

This is what the Sovereign LORD, the Holy One of Israel, says:

"In repentance and rest is your salvation,
in quietness and trust is your strength."

While there is certainly a time for achieving and working hard and earnestly striving for what is good, it is ultimately true that, in the reality of the spiritual life, there is strength in quietness and trust, there is rescue, there is deliverance, there is love and peace, guidance and protection, and all of what God brings in all of Who God is. So why is this verse tragic? Here's the end of verse 15:

but you would have none of it.

Isaiah goes on to describe the Israelites' predicament as they seek protection and rescue from an army. Can you relate? There are times when we place our sense of well-being in things or people other than God. It may even be something good, like a friendship, your family or even a ministry—but none of these things can give you true, lasting rest and strength.

■ What might those sources of protection or provision—other than God—be for you?

So what happened with the Israelites' misplaced trust?

> *You said, "No, we will flee on horses."*
> *Therefore you will flee!*
> *You said, "We will ride off on swift horses."*
> *Therefore your pursuers will be swift!*
> *A thousand will flee*
> *at the threat of one*
> *At the threat of five*
> *you will all flee away.* (Isaiah 30:16-17)

I do not believe God is directly causing these things to happen, but rather he is accurately predicting what will happen when his people rely on sources of strength other than himself. Listen to God's heart in this next verse:

> *Yet the LORD longs to be gracious to you;*
> *therefore he will rise up to show you compassion.*
> *For the LORD is a God of justice.*
> *Blessed are all who wait for him!* (Isaiah 30:18)

Did you know that is still true for you today? God actually longs to be something to you. What's keeping him back? Could it be said of you as well that "you would have none of it"?

■ Prayerfully ask God now: *Has this been true of me in any area? In what way?*

■ Why do you think you've resisted God's offer in that area of your life?

Each of us has areas of our lives in which we are running on our own power—a picture of life with Jesus that was never what God intended. One of the greatest challenges of the spiritual life, of life with God, is to learn the counterintuitive rhythms of repentance, rest, quietness, trust, *waiting*. This doesn't set us off on a passive journey but rather on a life of rich participation with God in the work he is doing here on Earth. We go as he calls. We stop when he warns. We yield. We work. All is in simple submission and surrender to his purpose, his voice, and all is accomplished in his power.

■ How do you find yourself responding to the idea of participating with God in this way?

Have you ever spent time with someone you knew didn't really want to be with you? Maybe a blind date gone wrong? Or a business meeting with a colleague who just didn't like you? Not very fun.

Growing up, my brothers had a term of endearment for such experiences when they happened in our family: Forced Family Fun. From time to time my idealistic parents would put forth a valiant effort to get themselves and all seven children to enjoy some meaningful family activity together. With children ranging in age from seventeen years to seventeen months (and with five rowdy boys in between) this was no easy task. While the events themselves are largely lost in memory to time, the one thing we all learned was that my parents were crazy—crazy to love us that much and crazy to think they could pull it off!

I doubt my parents found it funny at the time (as a parent myself, I know I wouldn't!), but now we all laugh hilariously when we remember those times. Forced Family Fun. Nothing could be truer.

For many people, the concept of spending time with God would fall solidly in the category of Forced Family Fun. We do it because we should; we know all the reasons it would be good for us, but the truth is that we dread it. It doesn't "fit" who we are or what our needs are, we do not look forward to it, and in the end we do it because we *have* to rather than because we *want* to.

Because we're so used to doing stuff we *have* to do—rather than doing things we *want* to do—we dutifully press on. But the vitality that could be there is never uncovered in the midst of our duty.

What would a "want to" connection with God be like? Surprisingly, one of the barriers that exists for us can be resistance: resistance to love, resistance to being unguarded and undefended in the presence of the One who truly loves us. Author Lynne Hybels created a piece of writing to invite us to that place. This is the kind of love Jesus offers.

"Let Me Love You"

Come away, God says. Yes, you, come away and sit with me. Come and let me give you the gift of my presence. I want to share the stillness of this moment with you. I want to whisper words of kindness to you. I want to pour my infinitely rich and deep love into your very soul.

So come, let me love you. Let me love that part of you that believes you are valuable only while you are serving others. You are valuable for just who you are. You don't have to keep running. You don't have to prove your worth through frantic activity. Let me love that part of you that is weary and needs to rest. Listen, listen as I tell you to drop your burdens right now, and rest like a child in the presence of a loving Father. . . .

So come. Sit with me. Let me love you. (© 2005 by Lynne Hybels <www.lynnehybels.com>)

The ability to sit "unagenda-ed" and undefended in the presence of God is something that we grow into. And like it or not, our capacity for intimacy and openness has often been developed in many human relationships prior to our relationship with God. Many of us learned to remain behind walls of defense—resolving never to trust in response to past hurts. Others appear open and transparent, when in reality their cheerful talk is just another mask that shields them from real vulnerability.

Overcoming years' worth of resistance to enter into intimacy with God is not quickly or easily done, but it is both essential and possible. We will need to learn new ways of being with God and with ourselves. Take some time to do a personal "intimacy inventory" reflecting on how you relate to both God and others.

■ How easy or hard is it for others to get to know the real you?

■ What factors have most strongly contributed to your capacity for intimacy in relationships?

■ What helps you to receive from others?

■ What things help you be willing to "sit down" in the chair and get quiet?

■ What helps you to "lean in" to God and pay attention?

■ What helps you receive from God?

Thus far we have discovered that our souls are living, and require nurture through authentic connection with God. Through that nurturing connection, our souls receive rest, healing, strength and power for transformation. But how do those connections with God happen? They are cultivated by the intentional, deliberate activity of carving out time and space to pay attention to and become open to this ongoing work of God in our lives. And when we carve out that time and space, it has the effect of helping us to "sit down" at the table with God, to "get quiet" and to "lean in" expectantly to receive what he has to offer our thirsty souls. We are no longer striving; we are resting and open.

"Be still, and know that I am God" (Psalm 46:10). That's how transformation takes place. I can't say what specific truth you need to hear, or in what area God has been moving you toward surrender—but I can promise that he brings quite a bit to the table and yet will not move until you bring what you and only you can: your willingness, brokenness and so on.

One of the most powerful forces to drive us toward the chair of transformation is painful circumstances in our lives. When we run out of options, when our plans are exposed as insufficient, when our best is just not good enough, we are more willing to sit down. That's why so many people turn to God initially in seasons of great pain—and it's why so many of us experience a depth of transformation when we endure such trials.

What if we could become the kind of people who are accustomed to meeting with God in a state of openness and surrender without having to be forced there by pain? What if we see the value and learn ways of going there voluntarily? Of course this will not eliminate those unavoidable times of pain in our lives, but the process of leaning in to God in the midst of them will be more natural.

> *It was good for me to be afflicted*
> *so that I might learn your decrees.*
> (Psalm 119:71)

> *My troubles turned out all for the best—*
> *they forced me to learn from your textbook.*
> (Psalm 119:71 *The Message*)

- Describe someone you know who experienced great hardship yet, as a result, also experienced intense spiritual growth.

- Has there been a time of personal pain for you that also spurred a season of growth? When? What happened?

As we move toward spiritual practices, you may find it takes enormous time and effort to abandon your everyday activities for a time and actually sit with God. That's okay. Even very small steps consistently made in the right direction will eventually get you to your destination. And the kinds of steps we will explore through this study series will be the kind that can fit in everyday life—you won't have to quit your job and enlist in a monastery! What we're really talking about here is a re-orientation of your life around the reality of the spiritual realm.

Eventually, it becomes a way of life—a way of being with ourselves, with God and with others; a way of remaining attuned to God, even in the midst of our activities. This way of life helps us care for our souls, and even, at times, for the souls of everyone around us.

■ What has been your experience with spiritual practices in the past? What form did they take?

What or who motivated you to embrace them?

Was it life-giving? Boring?

■ What is your current routine, if any? How effective at caring for your soul has it been?

■ In what area of your life would you *most* like your experience of God to increase?

The chair awaits you at all times.
Please, for your own sake, sit down.
Breathe deeply.
And let God love you.

Summary

Transformation occurs through a joint effort between God, who supplies the power, the love, the knowledge and the vision, and each one of us, who bring nothing more to the table than our openness and willingness. It can be helpful to actually picture a table at which God is always present and where we have the opportunity to sit down and receive from him what we need. Actually sitting down in an undefended way with God with no agenda, though, can be difficult to do. We may resist because time with God feels like an obligation or because we fear being that intimate and open. Despite our concerns, God longs for us to draw near—he desires to empower and heal and guide and bless and protect us. And the good news is, we can grow in our capacity to slow down enough to be with God through spiritual practices that over time become a way of life. A way of developing a "with-God" kind of life. The life of a well-cared-for soul.

Opening

What was a recent "table" that you sat down at? (Think, perhaps, of a team meeting or other planning session.) What did you "bring" to that table (for example, creativity, vision, an idea, an investment, a product)?

Discussion

1. What, if anything, did you sense God stirring in you through this third experience?

2. Go back over your written responses to parts one through four. What one or two ideas stand out as something you'd like to bring to the group? Why did they stand out to you?

3. Return to part one, "The Two Chairs." How did you respond to that metaphor? And how did you respond to the questions on pages 60-61?

4. Read Isaiah 30:15-18 out loud. God's people tragically placed their trust in things and people other than God, with dire consequences. What might be the top "god-substitute," for example wealth or prestige, that poses a similar temptation for you?

5. What would you say is one of your main barriers to intimacy with God? Is that barrier similar to barriers you face in other relationships? Why or why not?

6. What is your current "soul care" routine? What do you currently do to care for your soul? How would you like to see it change in the future, if at all?

Prayer

If space allows, place two empty chairs in the center of your discussion group. Assign one chair as the "God chair," and then take turns physically sitting down in the other, being mindful and aware of the feelings you have as you choose to sit down, as you let your body "get quiet" (watch out for shaking feet or hunched shoulders!), and then as you physically "lean in" toward the second chair.

From that seated position (or imagining yourself to be in such a chair) take turns closing the discussion time by speaking to God openly and honestly about your personal desire or resistance to sitting down in that chair. What do you want to say to him? Remember, remaining quiet is perfectly fine. It's OK to just let yourself feel what it feels like and rest in the fact that God already knows—and loves—your heart.

Before the next gathering, everyone should complete "Experience Four: Soul Decisions."

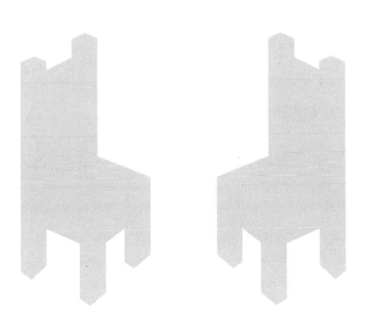

"A longing fulfilled is sweet to the soul."

PROVERBS 13:19

1 GLORY MOMENTS

Years after that episode at the sidelines of Heartbreak Hill, I had the opportunity to learn from some friends who actually had run the Boston Marathon. We were a group of women from a diverse set of spiritual backgrounds, with a diverse set of spiritual beliefs, coming together on a regular basis to explore what the Bible had to say about the spiritual life.

Our study one night centered around several verses that compared the spiritual life to a race:

Do you not know that in a race all the runners run, but only one gets the prize? Run in such a way as to get the prize. (1 Corinthians 9:24)

Let us run with perseverance the race marked out for us. (Hebrews 12:1)

With several accomplished runners in the room that night, I figured they could really help the rest of us out with this metaphor. "Tell us," I asked, "when you get to that point when you want so badly to give up, what do you do? How do you make it through the wall?" I had always wondered this, and figured I wasn't the only one. "Do you recall all the intense training and keep telling yourself you can do it?" I continued. "Do you see the people running with you and want to keep up? Do you hear the crowd cheering you on and make an extra effort to avoid embarrassment? Do you imagine the finish line—playing over the details of the finishing moment to keep your legs moving? How do you *do* it?"

Liz didn't even take a moment for reflection or consideration. "I know right away. I know exactly what those moments are and exactly what I need to do to make it through." We all leaned forward to hear what she had to say next (especially with all those race numbers and medals hanging on her wall!).

"You just take the next step. And then the next step. And the next step. When you can barely breathe anymore, when your legs are screaming with pain, when you mind is fuzzy and you want to give up, you need to take the next step. The crowd can't help you, the other runners become irrelevant, the end of the race is an eternity away. It's all about summoning the strength just to take one step."

That was not the answer I expected. Nor was it what anyone else expected, judging by the hush in the room. We were all thinking the same thing: *That's true in my life right now too.*

She understood the silence and went on, "Those are the glory moments, and they don't only come in running. Glory moments are when you're having an argument with someone you love—and everything in you wants to just slam the door and walk away. But you walk back and sit down. That's a glory moment.

"And when you're fighting against a temptation that's been knocking you out for years, and you say no: that's a glory moment. People often think that the finish line is the glory moment, but that's not really true.

"The glory moments are when you wanted to quit, and you kept going—when you took the next step."

I'm not telling this story to suggest that we should just try harder, instead of really connecting with God. The connection I want us to make is this: rather than focus on the finish line, each of us has the opportunity to take a next step. I'm not saying the next step is to run faster or harder. The marathon is life, remember. All the steps are figures of speech—the steps we take in life. For one person, the next step may simply be to assess soul health—and then just sit with that for awhile. Or a next step may be to take an honest look at what's at stake in life, and then undertake some dramatic rearranging in order to restore health and life to your soul. A next step could involve solidifying your relationship with this God who loves you and pursues your heart.

You can give up and head for the sidelines, or you can take a next step. It's your call.

Your glory moment is waiting.

■ Can you relate to the idea of a "glory moment"? Describe a time when you made a courageous "taking a next step" decision. What was that step, and what happened as a result?

We begin with vision.

Any form of change we undergo, Dallas Willard asserts in *Renovation of the Heart,* involves three factors: vision, intention and means. Vision is that picture of the preferred future—the way it *could* be if a change took place. Declaring our intention is essential: we move from thinking about a particular change to intending that change to occur. And the final factor, of course, is the means: the various processes we engage or resources we pursue in order to experience the change.

To illustrate this, he points to the "change" involved in learning a second language, and he contrasts two cultures. In the United States, we have virtually unlimited access to means which could support an intention to learn a second language besides English. We have an abundance of books, audiotape courses, classrooms, tutors we could hire, etc., but the fact is very few of our English-speaking citizens ever learn another language. Why? There's very little motivation. It's just not that important.

By contrast, people in many other areas of the world, and in particular some of the world's poorest nations, learn English. They have very few resources at their disposal—very little direct opportunity— yet they learn English. Why? Their motivation is clear. For them, learning English is the ticket to a better life—a ticket to a better future.

Without it, their prospects of earning a living and raising themselves out of poverty are slim. With English, they feel the world is opened up to them.

So what does that have to do with us as we discuss the soul? Everything. Most of us are surrounded by a relative abundance of resources to deepen the spiritual life. Bibles or books on prayer lay around unread, journals unused, church or other ministry gatherings unattended, worship music not listened to, and so on. So why are our souls so parched, so thirsty and dry even when surrounded by so much?

I can't help but think that, like me, many people have never so much as considered the health of their souls. And as a result, they have no vision of what could be different, much less have they declared an intention to live accordingly. So the means lie all around us, unused, unwanted. God himself remains in our world, but we don't pursue or engage him.

How about you? One of your next steps may be to see more clearly what *could* be.

■ Let your mind imagine for a few minutes: What would you want your experience of God to be like? Describe that picture.

Look back to your answers in part two of experience one, the soul neglect/soul health exercise. Reread your words above. Then prayerfully answer the questions on the next page.

■ What's at stake in your personal life?

■ What's at stake in your immediate family and with your circle of friends?

■ What's at stake in your area of work or other contribution to the world?

I think of it as taking the swan dive. Ever watch an Olympic diver do this very simple dive? It is elegant and beautiful, appearing deceptively easy. Your dive doesn't need to be that pretty. Mine certainly wasn't; mine was more like a duck dive. But no matter, the point is that I did it. I climbed up on that high platform and dove in.

To me, taking a swan dive symbolized a decision to abandon the ways of my past and to venture into a different kind of future. I longed for a deep relationship with God. I wanted to build a luxurious, relaxed, unhurried, no-holds-barred relationship of complete abandon with God. I needed to quit the illusion of giving to others when my soul was in fact so vacuous.

I felt a bit guilty at first, like I was letting the rest of my responsibilities go, trusting that if God intended those balls to stay in the air, there would be a way they would. And if they fell, then so be it. But my guilt was appeased by this Scripture, which ministered to me and I hope will challenge your willingness as well: "Above all else, guard your heart, / for everything you do flows from it" (Proverbs 4:23).

The words *heart* and *soul* could be used interchangeably in this context; the meaning is the same: protect your heart, your interior world. Guard your soul's health, for as we've seen, *everything* flows from there.

■ Paraphrase this verse from Proverbs with your name in the text, giving specific examples of the "else" priorities in your life and the recipients of the wellspring of your life.

Intention

This is not an admonition to quit your day job! This kind of relationship with God is nowhere and everywhere; it takes all your time and none of your time; it requires everything and nothing. It is organic, it is authentic, it emerges, it becomes. But it also requires a decision. Are you willing to take that swan dive? Are you willing to learn a new way? Is the vision of what could be clear enough in your mind yet? Are you able to count the cost? You will have many friends along this path, but you must choose it for yourself.

Your signature below reflects a personal commitment to prioritize the care of your soul:

_____

Means

For many of us, our next step might be exploring new means of connecting with God. I know this was an important facet in my journey. I explored new ways of mindfulness, new ways of prayer, new ways of being with God in his Word, new ways of relating, new ways of resting, new routines of withdrawing from my busy life and even a few new authors on the spiritual life to read.

The means of restoring your soul's health are as readily available as God's presence with you at all times is, and the resources for restoring your soul's health are designed to help your soul increase its connection with God. These kinds of helps include the Bible, other great books, study guides, retreats, seminars, church services, soul friends and mentors. The Soul Care study guides cover practices such as prayer, solitude, soul friends, Scripture reading, self-examination and simplicity.

■ What "means" do you already have in place to care for your soul?

■ Which of the three dimensions of spiritual practices is strongest in your life right now (large group, small group, individual)?

■ Which do you find yourself wishing was stronger? Why?

■ Do you sense God suggesting a next step for you in that area? If so, what is it?

So what happens now? You may be wondering if entering a season of spiritual self-care will result in self-absorption. That is certainly possible, but when openly and honestly pursued, this journey will not lead to self-absorption. It *cannot,* because becoming more like Jesus causes us to become more loving, not more self-focused. As we grow closer to the heart of God, we grow closer to his concerns for the world around us.

When you're living a life of vibrant intimacy with God, in fact, you cannot stop the power of God from working through you. You'll experience what Jesus said would happen: "I am the vine; you are the branches. If you remain in me and I in you, you will bear much fruit" (John 15:5). And the best news of all: your "fruit-bearing" won't suck the life out of you! It will energize you, because it comes out of the overflow of what's going on in your soul.

Take about five minutes to sit in complete silence. Even if you're in a crowded coffee shop or college dorm or your kids are playing in the next room, let your own internal noise get quiet. Sit down in that chair. Picture yourself leaning in; enjoy the silence; allow God to speak to your heart. Silently acknowledge his presence with you, express your gratitude for his love and then rest in the silence.

■ Is there anything in particular you sense he is saying to you? Can you discern any invitation from him? If so, respond to what you sense he's said. For example, if you've heard God reiterate his love for you personally, you could take this opportunity to let him know you'll receive that love or that you are grateful or hesitant or even afraid.

If you do not sense God's voice, please don't feel you need to invent something. Perhaps it is enough for you to sit quietly and simply reconnect with your desire to hear from God.

5 GROUP DISCUSSION

Summary

When we most want to quit but instead courageously take just one more step toward our destination, those steps are the "glory moments"—*soul decisions* that open doors of possibility that would otherwise be lost. In our relationship with God, those glory moments may take many forms. A small step to slow our pace of life, for instance, or a small step to actually listen to God, or a step to rest our bodies, even the smallest act of obedience—those are the soul decisions that set a steady course toward soul health. Some especially important steps are to allow ourselves to *see what could be,* to *set our intention* in that direction and then to *engage the means* of pursuing that destination. Over time as those steps are taken, it is entirely possible and even quite natural to experience the quality of life that Jesus made available to us—and then, to have that life flow through us into the hearts and souls of those around us.

Opening

Tell a story on yourself. What's a relatively insignificant area of personal growth in which you had ample means but never made progress (like the set of Pilates tapes you purchased at 1 a.m. from an infomercial that have yet to be opened)?

Discussion

1. What, if anything, did you sense God stirring in you through this fourth experience?

2. Go back over your written responses to parts one through four. What one or two ideas stand out as something you'd like to bring to the group? Why did they stand out to you?

3. Return to the first question in part two, "Getting the Vision," and share your response with the group: What would you want your experience of God to be like? Describe that picture.

4. Some of us have had the privilege of knowing someone who represented the "swan dive" kind of abandon to God. If you know someone like that, who is it? What do you know (or imagine) motivates them and sustains them in that way of life?

5. Which of the three expressions of spiritual practices—large group, small group or individual—comes most naturally for you? Which would you like to explore further in the future? What might be a reasonable next step for you?

6. Tell the group about your experience in part four of having five minutes of silence in which you invited God to speak. Did you sense anything? How did you respond? If you didn't sense anything, how did you respond to that?

A fun but meaningful closing exercise would be to provide clay or another artistic medium and take about a half hour to create something that physically represents the way you'd like to experience your relationship with God in the future.

Prayer

If you feel comfortable, close this time in prayer, thanking God for the gift of your relationships with each other and asking his help and guidance in these matters in the future.

CONCLUSION

You can finish this race. You can experience the quality of life available in a relationship with God. You can experience hope and freedom and purpose and transformation and have a meaningful impact on the world around you. You can even make it up your own Heartbreak Hill.

Whatever steps lie ahead for you, however big or small, remember to recognize them as the glory moments they are. Honor each and every one. In your exhaustion or enthusiasm, in your depletion or strength, in your pain or pleasure, or fear or joy, you can just take a next step. And a next one. And then a next one.

Slowly but surely your soul will be restored by the God who loves you and draws you close, pouring his living water into the depths of who you are. Practically speaking, you might want to explore additional resources such as the Soul Care Resources guide *Spiritual Friendship* or other books on the spiritual life, and visit <www.soul care.com>.

Care for your soul, and you won't be able to stop what God intends to do through you!